Published by:

Writer's Publishing House

Prescott, AZ 86301

Paperback ISBN: 978-1-64873-557-8

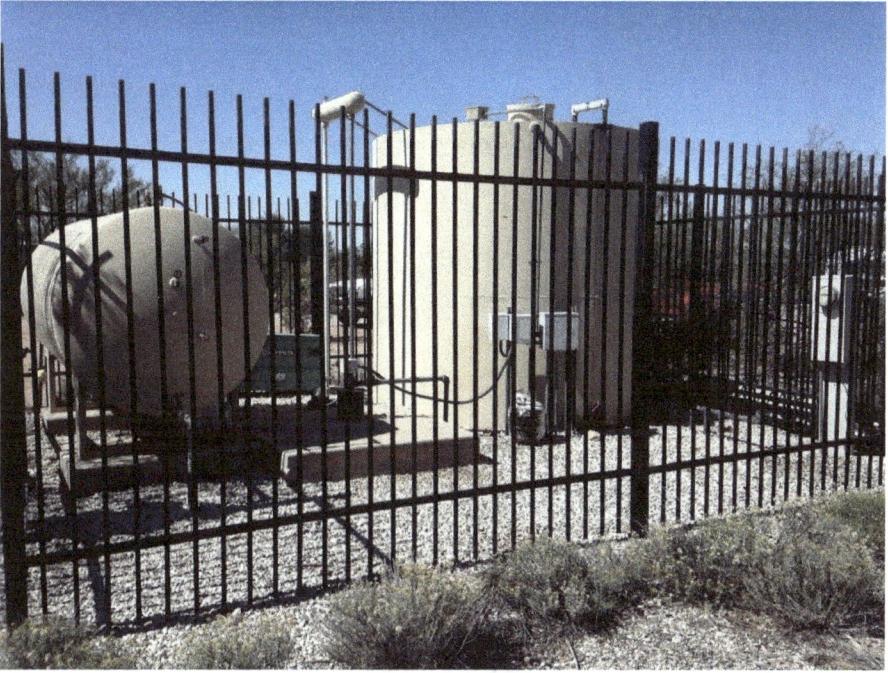

GROUNDWATER-SHARING CONTRACTS

Formerly Called

Well Share Agreements

By

Gary L. Hix, R.G.

Foreword

The concept presented here is deliberately called groundwater-sharing contracts—and not "well share agreements"—because it introduces a more accurate, groundbreaking approach to sharing groundwater between two or more properties.

Traditional agreements often mis-characterized the arrangement by focusing on the "well" rather than the true resource being shared: the groundwater itself. What was commonly labeled a simple "agreement" was, in reality, a binding legal contract with profound, long-term consequences for real property rights and property values.

Many homeowners discovered these impacts the hard way, especially those whose homes depended on a shared well located on someone else's land. A fundamental shift in the approach to groundwater sharing is urgently needed to better protect homebuyers, lenders, and all parties involved in properties that rely entirely on groundwater originating from another parcel.

The Fundamental Distinction: Wells vs. Groundwater

Groundwater is a vital resource used daily, delivered through a water well. Legally and practically, a water well is a permanent improvement that becomes part of the real property. From the perspective of a former well-drilling contractor who has designed, drilled, and equipped countless wells; once constructed, a water well cannot be relocated. It remains fixed to the land and can reliably produce groundwater for 50 years or longer.

Groundwater itself however, is treated differently under most state laws. It is not real property, but a dynamic commodity constantly in slow motion beneath the surface. The water under a property today may be gone tomorrow, influenced by weather patterns, aquifer recharge rates, and pumping from nearby wells. Even in states that follow the "ownership" doctrine—declaring groundwater beneath the land belongs to the surface owner—there is no guarantee that any usable water exists. As hydrogeologists confirm, vast areas of land simply lack accessible groundwater.

The Reality of Importing Groundwater

When a parcel has no viable groundwater, building a habitable home requires importing water from another property. Some states mandate that captured groundwater be put to "beneficial use" on the land where it was extracted. Strictly interpreted, this would prohibit sharing with neighboring parcels—yet shared systems have operated for decades under the guise of "well share agreements.

The critical oversight in many older agreements was this: it was never truly the well-being shared, but the groundwater. This distinction was rarely properly addressed, leading to unclear rights, unequal burdens, and potential disputes. Modern contracts must explicitly recognize and clarify groundwater as the shared resource to ensure fair, sustainable arrangements for the future.

The Need for Formal Groundwater-Sharing Contracts

Homeowners on water-scarce land must enter into a formal contract with the owner of a property where groundwater is legally captured and recovered. Once extracted, that groundwater becomes the personal property of the landowner where the well is located. Parties must then agree on, execute, and record a detailed contract specifying how the groundwater will be shared.

Call for Broader Recognition and Reforms

The concept of groundwater-sharing should be brought to the attention of groundwater regulators, professional trade organizations, FHA and VA loan underwriters, the National Association of Realtors, and lawmakers.

In many states, there are minimal regulations protecting the health, safety, and welfare of buyers purchasing homes on shared wells. Currently, water well drillers, pump installers, real estate professionals, homeowners, mortgage lenders, well inspectors, and lawyers play roles in this area.

Advocacy is needed for:

- Standardization of physical water well inspections and adoption of minimum water quality standards for "potable" water.

- The introduction of professional, licensed water well inspectors qualified to evaluate groundwater-sharing contracts and the quality of captured groundwater.

- Training, testing, licensing, and regulation of water well inspectors, similar to other professionals serving real estate buyers (e.g., real estate professionals, home inspectors, pest and septic inspectors).

- Clear guidelines for FHA and VA loan underwriters on required well inspections and testing measures.

- Assurance for buyers that private or shared wells will provide safe, potable, and sustainable groundwater for a reasonable period.

State regulators should recognize that inspecting water wells for property sales and transfers is a consulting service—not a routine service call or contracting work. Water well inspectors should be licensed accordingly.

Federal agencies overseeing loans must recognize that their requirements for approval are not practical to apply in the field.

Lawyers who draft groundwater-sharing documents need to recognize that changes are needed in their contracts. Existing shared well managers require better education of their responsibilities and liabilities in managing this precious and essential commodity; groundwater,

Contents

Purpose

Series Background and Evolution

This Revised Edition (2026) updates and expands upon the author's earlier works in a continuing series that first addressed the subject of *Well Share Agreements.* The topic was initially introduced in Chapter 5 of *Domestic Water Wells in Arizona: A Guide for Realtors,*[1] and explored in greater depth in the follow-up publication, *Well Share Agreements: A Guide for Well Managers* [2] and the first version of: *Groundwater-Sharing Contracts, Formerly Called: Well Share Agreement.*[3]

Substantial portions of those earlier materials have been revised and incorporated into this latest edition.

Across the United States, shared water wells remain a common practice, yet clear guidance on their proper structure, management, and the causes of their frequent breakdowns continues to be limited.

---

[1] Chapter 5 of *Domestic Water Wells in Arizona: A Guide for Realtors*
[2] *Well Share Agreements: A Guide for Well Managers*, E-Book, Amazon 2019, G. Hix.
[3] *Groundwater-Sharing Contracts, Formerly Called: Well Share Agreement.* E-Book, Amazon 2023, G. Hix.

Water well-sharing arrangements remain in everyday use throughout the nation, little has been written until now about how they should work and why they sometimes fail.

Substantial content from those earlier works incorporates into this Revised Edition (2026).

Purpose and Intended Audience

- Hard copy publication introduces the subject of groundwater-sharing and intends to:
- Help real estate professionals explain to buyers what purchasing a home on a shared well provides.
- Clarify for homeowners what the clauses in their shared well agreements mean.
- Help water well inspectors explain well agreements to buyers when inspecting a shared well.
- Assist developers planning to use a shared domestic water well for their new development.
- Assist lawyers in creating better worded groundwater-sharing contracts.

The publication informs homeowners, real estate professionals, water well inspectors, and other interested parties. It is not intended to provide legal advice concerning groundwater law or contractual matters. Rather, it serves as a written account of lessons learned by someone who has worked closely with individuals caught in difficult circumstances—often unaware of how they arrived there or how to resolve the issues within their well share agreements.

Goals and Key Focus Areas

The goal of this publication is to help resolve many of the conflicts that arise from poorly written well shared agreements.

It emphasizes the critical importance of identifying the legal source of groundwater when drafting a contract designed to share it. The text also explains why careful framing and precise wording are essential to protect the rights and interests of all parties involved. Ultimately, one must ask what is the true value of a home served by a shared well if the contract cannot provide legal access to groundwater and secure each homeowner's rightful share?

Additional Hopes and New Content

There is also hope this publication will encourage professional water well inspectors to evaluate groundwater-sharing contracts on behalf of homebuyers. The revision introduces Chapter 13, which presents essential information every current and prospective shared well manager should understand about the duties and responsibilities of their volunteer role.

Acknowledgments

I am forever indebted to my wonderful wife, Marilyn, who has stood by me day and night, patiently enduring countless discussions and reviews of the many questions and issues raised in this book about groundwater-sharing. My heartfelt appreciation also extends to the many friends who have listened endlessly to my thoughts on this subject, as well as to the readers of my earlier works and the homeowners who have faced the challenges of living with a shared water well. My time and effort will not be in vain if this publication helps more people recognize the importance of addressing this often overlooked yet critical gap in real estate transactions.

Chapter One

Why Groundwater-Sharing Contracts?

Figure 1 An example of a groundwater-sharing system nicely constructed and protected.

This revised edition, begins by taking exception to words used in the past to describe shared well agreements or well share agreements and now introduces the concept of calling these documents groundwater-sharing contracts because that is precisely what they are. Calling them groundwater-sharing contracts is far more representative of the true purpose of these documents. They are legal contracts between two or more parties intended to define the sharing of groundwater from a water well.

Defining the Contract Precisely

If the intent is to share groundwater derived from a well, then call it a groundwater-sharing contract of private property taken from a permitted water source or aquifer. Many states use the term registration for a legally permitted well and require that it be registered with them in the name of the legal landowner. Some states require the landowner to possess a state-granted or water district groundwater right associated with an aquifer and parcel of land. Any groundwater-sharing contract should be based on a document establishing that the shared groundwater was legally captured.

Legal Validity and Breach Protection

For a groundwater-sharing contract to withstand a breach of contract complaint, the shared commodity must have been obtained legally. Courts in all states would hesitate to render a decision on a contract for an illegally obtained commodity. This minor detail was often ignored in many past well-sharing agreements when the well permit, or the granted groundwater right, was not identified in the agreement.

Common Flaws in Earlier Agreements

Many earlier agreements only defined the real property upon which the well was drilled, but groundwater is no longer part of the land in most states. Other well sharing agreements described the water source being shared as coming from an easement. An easement, however, is a non-possessory interest in real property that grants other landowners the right to use a portion of another person's land for a specific purpose.

The grantors of these earlier documents often agreed only to share their interest in the well or the real property. However, "There is no property in groundwater until it is captured" is a stated concept of water law that groundwater is not real property in most states.[4] More about groundwater law in other states follows in Chapter 5.

Need for Clear Identification of the Legal Source

As a result of research on the subject of who owns the groundwater that is being shared under these older contracts, the concept is introduced that there is a genuine need for identification and clarification of the legal source of the groundwater being shared. It could be either the registration of the well or a "water right" granted to extract a specific amount

---

[4] Who Owns the Water? A publication of Water Systems Council, 2016.

of groundwater from a given aquifer. The right to capture, divert, hold, and share this most precious resource needs to be identified up front in the contract before offering to share it with others.

Imperfection of Contracts and Real-World Disputes

Past involvement with disputes over issues in shared well agreements leads to the statement that there is no perfect contract. No matter how many clauses are put into a contract meant to handle daily operations, something at a later date will trigger a dispute that was not clearly defined in the contract.

Finally, to strengthen the case for changes, true stories about groundwater agreements learned through experience dealing with them daily will be shared. Many shared well members just needed some guidance to help them resolve issues that arose within their agreements. Some issues brought forward required mediation, while others were solved through court action. A genuine need exists for this book in hopes of preventing future problems with the sharing of groundwater.

Chapter Two

Examining Existing Well Share Agreements

Initial Review as a Title Examiner

First step involves examining the document from the perspective of a former title examiner because it impacts real property, real estate sales, transfers, and financing. Initial focus centers on evidence that the groundwater-sharing agreement has been recorded in the county where the well and the property are located. Next, confirmation occurs that the document has been signed by the grantor and the grantee(s) who intended to share the groundwater. A proper groundwater-sharing contract must have been signed by all parties, signatures must have been properly notarized, and the document must be recorded in the county where the well is located.

Assessing Document Quality

If all elements prove satisfactory to that point, the entire document receives reading and grading according to the scale from the first published paper on this subject: *Well Share Agreements, The Good, The Bad, and The Ugly.*[5] A once-over

---

[5] Groundwater Well: Use and Shared Use Agreements, The Good, The Bad, and The Ugly, G. Hix, Lorman Education Services, Symposium, Tucson, AZ. Sept. 27, 2007.

review of the document reveals whether it contains sufficient clauses to address critical aspects of groundwater management—from legal capture to proportional payment by each party for their share of that most precious commodity.

Classification After Grading

After grading the document as good, bad, or ugly, classification follows into one of four types of groundwater-sharing agreements as defined below.

Conceptual Models for Groundwater-Sharing Agreements

Overview of the Four Models

Listed below are four primary structural forms into which well share agreements, or groundwater-sharing contracts, can be categorized:

A. **Party Wall Agreement:** 50-50 ownership, equal benefits, equal maintenance & liabilities.

B. **Condominium-HOA:** Common property, management oversight, owner responsibilities.

C. **Small Business Model:** LLC or Co-Op, employee owned, structure, voting members, rules.

D. **Public Water Supply:** If greater than 14 homes. Regulated by local health depts. Selling water in bulk quantities with no ownership of groundwater.

Each model would have specific clauses necessary to accomplish the desired needs for the operation and proper system management. Sharing the groundwater proportionally and sharing the "ownership" of the physical components of the complete water system requires very different clauses. The sharing of groundwater is best done in terms of the volume each member uses monthly while the sharing of maintenance and repair costs should be shared equally periodically or when necessary.

Figure 2 An example of a two-party shared well system for summer homes in the mountains.

Model A: Party Wall Agreement

Core Characteristics

If the nature of the agreement is a Model A as shown in the list above, it will read much like a party wall agreement. Each party will have an equal, but undivided ownership interest in and to all system components. All parties would share an undivided interest in and to the individual water lines serving each parcel, or the distribution lines can be owned individually so that each owner is responsible for maintaining their individual water line.

A statement should be made that this was the intent of the agreement.

Under a party wall type of agreement, all parties share an undivided interest in and to a defined portion of the land upon which the system has been built, typically described as the "well site". The Party Wall Agreement structure concept is that all parties share ownership, maintenance responsibility, and liabilities equally.

Practical Implications

Under this model, both parties will likely render equal monthly or annual payments regardless of how much water each party uses. Water meters are not typically installed in this model. Both parties hold undivided but equal ownership of the groundwater captured by the well. Obviously two parties sharing one water well must be good neighbors for all times. If one parcel is sold, the new owner must be a good neighbor also. If the electrical meter for operating the well is permitted in the homeowner's name with the well and it also serves his/her home, splitting power service costs proportionally can become an issue.

Model B: Condominium-HOA Style

Partial ownership, conceptual Model B is much like living in a Condominium complex. Rather than owning and operating the system on a 50-50 basis, members hold only a vested interest in the water system and pay a fee for the proportional amount of groundwater they use. This model works best if each member has a working water meter. A well-manager or Well Owners Association maintains and manages the central portion of the system, but individual members have responsibilities to maintain their own portion of the overall system. Each member may share an undivided interest in the common grounds or equipment but still be responsible for their own water delivery lines.

Model C: Small Business Structure

Organizational Setup

Conceptual Model C is where the groundwater-sharing system is structured much like a small business and is managed as if it were one. This model uses a state-registered name for the managing association. It is typically structured as a limited liability company, a partnership, or a Co-op. It places the ownership of the parcel that the well is located on in the name of the business group. The water diversion point (well registration or groundwater right) is also registered with the granting or controlling agency in the name of the small business. The electrical power service contract for the well and any booster or water treatment equipment is also listed in the same business name. This structure is preferred if not required for buyers seeking FHA and VA loans.

Operational Details

The contract is titled and worded between the small business and the individual members sharing the water. Each property owner in this model will also have a working water meter. In this model, the small business or Co-op has ownership of the captured groundwater being shared. Finally, a business checking account requiring two signatures in the name of the small business is established for holding receipts and dispersing payments to contractors and vendors. Structured in this manner, lenders are more likely to approve a loan application for a property on a shared well, even if it shares water with over four homes.

Model D: Public Water Supply System

Regulatory Framework

The conceptual Model D is, in fact, a public water supply system. A water system with over fourteen homes, or more than a total of twenty-five people, receiving their drinking water from a single water well automatically falls under the control of the EPA or the local health authority as a public water system. In the D model, the legally established entity owning the well and equipment is the same entity of record at the regulatory agency. Under the D model, the managing group must adhere to various US EPA water system operation rules and water quality testing requirements. This form must also retain a state or local designated water plant operator for system operation and water quality control.

Member Role and Distinctions

The first three models are under a contract to share the groundwater and operating expenses with others proportionally, while a member of the public water supply model gets their water under a water service agreement. Each property in this model must have a working water meter. They pay a fee for their water with little or no interest in real or personal property and are not involved with the management of the system. The public model wholly owns all captured groundwater, which it sells as a bulk commodity to members for a fee.

Key Distinction and Variations

To call it a "Well Share Agreement" under any of the first three models is a misnomer because these documents are contracts to share groundwater. There may be slight variations of what has been outlined above from state to state because of different concepts of groundwater law, contract law, and community or public water systems.

Some states refer to small water systems as "Community Water Wells" and some define them as any system having over four homes sharing one well. Shared wells or community wells share groundwater under the terms of a written contract.

Defining all the variations that might impact the formulation of a groundwater-sharing contract in each state is beyond the scope of this book.

Declarations of Covenants, Conditions and Restrictions

An additional attempt to establishing an agreement to share groundwater has been the use of a Declaration of CC&Rs. It's favored by mini developers who own all the designated parcels that would be sharing the benefits of a single domestic water well once they are sold. CC&Rs apply to the title of all parcels designated in the document once the document has been recorded.

The same qualifications would apply to CC&R's as to well share agreements. Is the legal source of groundwater specifically mentioned and is the intent to share groundwater, and not real property, clearly set forth? Remembering there is no property in groundwater until it is "legally" captured. (*emphasis added*). Can groundwater be reserved and held for future disbursement and use? That is the question with the use of CC&Rs?

Further, there is an appearance for this type of document to be more of a "take-it-or-leave-it" offer than a consensual agreement and it's certainly not a contract.

Chapter Three

Well Share Agreements Were Groundwater-Sharing Contracts

Figure 3 An example of a groundwater-sharing system designed to serve a number of homes.

Defining a Water Well and Its Legal Implications

A water well is a permanent improvement to real property installed by a licensed drilling contractor. A water well can also be defined as an artificial structure in the earth that an appropriate agency has "permitted" the landowner to install to divert and capture groundwater for beneficial use. When groundwater is legally captured and used for permitted purposes, the groundwater extracted via the well becomes more like private property that can then be shared. A more logical and accurate term for those documents would have been to label them as "Groundwater-sharing Contracts".

Shortcomings in Earlier Agreements

Many earlier sharing agreements were quite specific about describing the parcel of land on which the water well was located, and the parcel(s) of land being served the water but failed to mention the legal permit or appropriated water right to obtain the groundwater. Many agreements went to great lengths to define the equipment to be shared, such as the well, storage tanks, booster pumps, pressure tanks, and other equipment installed on the well owner's property. Under these agreements, members actually held an undivided interest in real property improvements.

Questioning Ownership of Groundwater

How strong is the argument that each member has an undivided interest in groundwater if the contract refers only to the real property, improvements, and easements on and over another's real property?

No Generic Agreements Exist

Parties needing to establish a new water-sharing agreement often ask if there is a generic version of an agreement that they can copy and fill in the blanks. Answer is always NO. Any groundwater-sharing contract must be custom-built around the legal source of water, the parties' desires, and the management style that the parties wish to create.

It should match what kind of sharing agreement they want: a party wall, a condominium, or an employee-owned business. There are many questions of ownership, responsibilities, management criteria, and duties of the well manager to resolve before words can be put into a written contract.

Chapter Four

What is Groundwater?

Evolution of Groundwater Understanding

Groundwater once viewed simply as underground rivers or vast subterranean oceans. Hydrogeologists have refined this understanding to where groundwater science now stands as a recognized professional discipline.

Courts could adopt the same scientific framework as hydrogeologists when addressing groundwater ownership and management.

Groundwater and Surface Water Connect in Numerous Ways:

- Gaining streams draw water from groundwater.
- Losing streams recharge groundwater.
- Some streams lose all surface flow to groundwater recharge and disappear entirely.
- Defining whether water is surface water or groundwater is a science not understood by all.

Surface water and groundwater remain interconnected. State laws must recognize and incorporate this reality when adjudicating legal cases involving groundwater sharing.

Current State of Court Rulings on Shared Wells

To date, hardly any significant court rulings involving groundwater have focused on domestic water wells or groundwater-sharing contracts. Shared well cases are argued under contract law terms rather than groundwater law. Most private and shared water wells are classified as exempt from groundwater rights laws. This classification does not mean that cases have never entered state court jurisdiction involving a well agreement.

For this reason, an effective groundwater-sharing contract should clearly state what was, or currently is, the legally permitted groundwater right and to whom it was issued.

Future Challenges and Regulatory Changes

In the future, many states could face pressure to restrict groundwater rights because of severe drought, land subsidence, and other emergencies. During severe droughts, a state water regulatory agency could mandate restrictions on groundwater extractions, including exempted wells being shared. If all exempt wells were required to reduce pumping by 20 percent, each member of a shared well system would face a proportionally greater reduction.

For states that follow the groundwater law known as "first in time, first in right", newer wells may need to be shut down to preserve rights of older wells. States may need to consider the highest and best use of water and reinterpret fundamental groundwater laws for the benefit of all citizens.

Ongoing Conflicts and Broader Implications

Conflict may always exist between long-held private ownership rights and governing agencies implementing policies for sustainable management of this most precious natural resource. Water rights, water sharing, water management, water pollution, and sustainability remain constant topics in the news. Everyone holds an interest in water because water is necessary for survival. State laws define water rights unless federal-reserved water rights are involved.

Scope Limitations

Water rights on federal property and Native American lands are not part of this discussion.

Chapter Five

Basic Groundwater Laws Across the Nation

Most states have adopted one of five general rules for the ownership and management of groundwater. Only one of the five rules maintains that groundwater is real property, and that rule is called "Absolute Dominion". States like Maine, Texas, Georgia, and a few others have held to this rule as best as possible. However, those states have made concessions to this theory for legal, environmental, and sustainable groundwater management considerations.

Groundwater law classifications roughly follow five different long-standing "rules" of law:[6]

1. Absolute Dominion Rule
2. Reasonable Use Rule
3. Prior Appropriation Doctrine
4. Correlative Rights Doctrine
5. Restatement of Torts Rule

---

[6] Who Owns the Water? A publication of Water Systems Council, 2016., Comparison of Groundwater Rights in the US a Lesson for Texas, Sanjaya Raj Joshi, Texas Tech Univ. MS Thesis. 2005.

A Primer on Groundwater Law, Joseph W. Dellapenna, 49 Idaho Law Review. 265, (2013).

A summary of each rule illustrates fundamental differences and approaches to managing groundwater and, occasionally, its relationship to surface water, from which some of these rules were derived.

Absolute Dominion Rule

The Absolute Dominion Rule is applied most strictly in Texas, Maine, and Indiana, and, to some extent, in Connecticut, Massachusetts, Rhode Island, Georgia, Louisiana, Minnesota, and Mississippi. It attempts to attach groundwater to the land even though groundwater constantly flows into and out of a given parcel of land and across local and state boundaries.

It had been referred to as the 'law of the biggest pump' until states added an exception that if pumping was malicious, actions could be taken against the landowner.

Reasonable Use Rule

The Reasonable Use Rule is endorsed in seventeen states, in both the East and West. This rule limits a landowner's access to beneficial use having a relationship to the use of the land. Off-site uses of groundwater are generally not permitted. A strict interpretation of this law would prohibit sharing of groundwater on multiple lots, if not because domestic wells are usually considered exempt from groundwater management laws.

Potential Changes Due to Drought

That exemption could be changed in the face of a severe or extended drought that required all groundwater pumping to be reduced. A groundwater-sharing contract would be subject to such a mandated reduction.

Prior Appropriation Doctrine

The Prior Appropriation Doctrine is used mainly in Western states, and it follows from old-world Spanish laws where "first in time is first in line". It was frequently used in early mining camps as the law of mineral rights. It is the most common law used to manage surface water rights, even if the state uses a different law for managing groundwater. Under Prior Appropriation, groundwater use is limited to reasonable and beneficial uses.

States that have adopted the Prior Appropriation rule to apply to major groundwater users do not apply it to domestic wells, except Utah, where a water right is needed for an exempt well. Exempt wells must be registered in states that adopted the Prior Appropriation Doctrine.

Correlative Rights Doctrine

The Correlative Rights Doctrine is based on the Reasonable Use Rule. Still, it differs in that it does not prohibit off-site uses. When pumping conflicts with neighboring users, it diverges to a proportionality rule established by the courts. This rule is used in California, Hawaii, Iowa, Oklahoma, and Tennessee. The understanding of this rule is that allocation of the state's groundwater is vested in the courts.

Restatement of Torts Rule

The Restatement of Torts Rule states that a landowner has use of groundwater on the land. As long as it benefits the land, a landowner is not liable for interfering with groundwater use by others. There are three exceptions to not being held liable for interfering with other users with the same rights:

1. Lowering the water table or artesian head pressures
2. Excessive withdrawal of groundwater on the local supply
3. Excessive groundwater withdrawals that directly impact surface waters
4. This rule has been adopted by only two states: Ohio and Wisconsin.

State Variations and Practical Application

Individual states might claim favoritism toward one of these five rules of law classifications, but in practice, their courts may have distorted or modified the principal groundwater law in one way or another. Most precedent-setting groundwater cases were about overuse of the natural resource or causing damages to a neighboring property while taking groundwater for state-approved uses.

A few cases in some western states have involved impacts of groundwater on surface water-supported environments, and a few have pitted state laws against federally reserved water rights or EPA-adopted rules.

Implications for Groundwater-Sharing Contracts

Any groundwater-sharing contract must fit within the water rights and contract laws of the state where the well and property are located. What makes a good contract in one state may not be acceptable in another state.

The basis of some groundwater laws goes back to old English or Spanish common laws for surface water that have been modified and adapted by the courts as scientific understanding of groundwater evolves. In most states, groundwater laws today are a "work in progress" as efforts continue to determine best management practices for everyone.

What makes a proper groundwater-sharing contract can be elusive and interpretative, given variations in state laws.

Chapter Six

When Purchasing a Property on a Shared Water Well

Prevalence of Private and Shared Wells in the US

The National Groundwater Association (NGWA) reports that 43 million US residents rely on domestic private water wells for drinking water.[7] Sales and purchases of properties occur every day, but only a select few involve rural properties that rely on a domestic water well. Fewer sales still involve properties sharing groundwater collected from one of these wells.

Disclosure Challenges in Real Estate Listings

The listing of a desirable property may not indicate that the drinking water source will be a single domestic water well and that sharing will occur with several other homes. If the listing does not disclose this, the seller's disclosure statement must disclose it. If the seller indicates that the home will be served by a shared water well, explanation of exactly what that means must fall to someone besides the Realtor.

---

[7] National Groundwater Association (NGWA) Groundwater Facts. www.ngwa.org

Implications for First-Time Well Users

What would such an explanation mean to a person who had never lived in a home relying on a groundwater well? Real estate professionals should always advise buyers to have the water system inspected before making an offer on a home. A professional water well inspector should provide information about the overall system and the contract for sharing groundwater.

Limitations in Current Inspections

The strength of a homeowner's claim to groundwater on a shared well depends solely on the words contained in the contract. The fact remains that most water well inspectors lack training to evaluate a shared well contract.

Figure 4 An example of a desert home that could be on a shared water well.

Role of Mortgage Lenders and Federal Underwriters

Mortgage lenders and federal underwriters like HUD, FHA, and VA hold vested interests in homes they finance. Underwriters apply new qualifications and criteria for validating a legal source of water for the home they insure.

Evolving Requirements and Impacts

Rules and minimum requirements for homes on shared water wells have tightened in recent years to the extent that homes purchased in the past and previously qualified no longer qualify because of the structure and wording of their well agreements. This book explains federal underwriter requirements and how some existing sharing agreements need modification to meet the new tighter underwriter requirements.

Chapter Seven Real Estate Professional

Do Not Evaluate Well Share Agreements

Limitations in Real Estate Education on Well-Sharing

The curriculum of most real estate schools around the US lacks sufficient time in allotted hours of instruction for a realtor's license to cover details of well-sharing agreements. Overall, real estate sales involving well-sharing agreements occur far less often and represent only a tiny percentage of total sales during the career of most agents. Much of this stems from the fact that well sharing occurs far more often in rural areas where groundwater is scarce or found only at great depths. Thus, no justification exists for core curriculum courses to allocate time to these contracts.

Importance in Well-Dependent Regions

However, many states contain counties almost entirely dedicated to private water wells as the principal source of domestic water for single-family homes. If the principal source of domestic water comes from a shared well and the client purchases only a small share of that resource, these contracts become critically important. Buyers of homes on shared wells deserve clear explanation of the terms of their agreement/contract.

Focus of Real Estate Training

In most real estate schools, time dedicates to core courses for new real estate agents on contracts for selling and transferring real estate. The two central contracts are the documents agents use for their services and the contract between seller and buyer. Both receive serious attention, with many test questions on various aspects of these documents.

Critical Perspective on Water Contracts

From this perspective, water remains an absolute requirement for life and to make any house a home. Therefore, any contract that grants or limits a homeowner's right to receive domestic water deserves the closest scrutiny.

Marketing Practices and Disclosures

When a realtor lists a home for sale, suggestions often go to the seller to promote the best and most desirable aspects of the home and property. Photographs capture the best eye-appeal aspects of the property, views from all points of the home, charming ambiance of the neighborhood, and proximity to schools and shopping. Seldom does it mention that the home is on a shared well despite its importance to prospective buyers.

Sellers must disclose specific features of the home and history of events occurring in and to the home and property. The number one feature requiring disclosure in any detailed listing is the source of water for the home.

Often, nothing more is said about the water source being a shared water well until close to the closing date, when a lawyer, escrow agent, or title company requires all relevant documents.

Timing of Key Discoveries

This timing typically reveals to the buyer's agent the significance of a shared water well inspection and obtaining a working copy of the groundwater agreement. Surprise may also arise that water quality testing must occur and receive acceptance by the lender before closing. Water quality sampling and testing require performance by licensed professionals. Tests can prove expensive, and testing laboratories need time to complete tests and certify results.

Realtor Responsibilities and Fiduciary Duty

Real estate professionals hold no obligation to discover or disclose adverse factors not reasonably apparent to someone with expertise only in real estate sales. However, real estate professionals maintain a fiduciary duty to act in their client's best interest.[8] This duty should interpret as possessing sufficient knowledge to recommend a shared well inspection, including evaluation of the shared well agreement.

---

[8] A Realtor's Duty to Refer a Competent Professional, Arizona Journal of Real Estate & Business. December 2023, Vol. 38 No.12.

Need for Specialized Well Inspections

Reference to the fiduciary responsibility of a real estate agent calls for a water well inspection for the buyer anytime the water source for a home comes from a shared water well. This raises the issue prevalent in almost all states; there is an absence of a recognized business or trade for performing water well inspections for sale and transfer of real estate, unlike home inspectors. A water well contractor most often provides this service.

Limitations of Current Providers

It proves fair to state that most water well and pump installation contractors lack training to evaluate a shared well agreement. More about performing well inspections appears below.

Chapter Eight

Who Performs Shared Well Inspections

Figure 5 Author inspecting and sampling the groundwater supplying a shared well system.

Current Practices in Water Well Inspections

In almost all states, water well inspections are performed by domestic well pump installers who are contractors. While well and pump contractors may know how to install and repair groundwater pumping equipment, virtually none are trained to evaluate a groundwater-sharing contract properly.

Defining Water Well Inspection for Real Estate

Definition begins with what a water well inspection for the sale and transfer of real estate is and is not. Performing the service and rendering a written report to individuals contemplating purchasing real estate supported by a domestic water well is not contracting and is not a service call. It is consulting!

Comparison with Other Inspection Professions

Appraisers, home Inspectors, pest inspectors, and even septic tank inspectors are all licensed or certified professionals whose trade requires qualifications and testing. However, no such requirement exists for being a water well inspector. No job description exists for a water well or shared well inspector to evaluate a shared well agreement. For rural buyers in most states, "caveat emptor" applies regarding shared water wells.

Importance as Consulting Services

The service of performing a water well inspection for someone who possibly has never lived on a property solely supported by a domestic water well constitutes a vitally important decision-making service that fits the definition of consulting. How many water well drillers and pump installation contractors perform well inspections for home buyers without being qualified, certified, or licensed to consult?

Advocacy for Professional Water Well Inspectors

This book endeavors to make the case for establishing professional water well inspectors to be consulted for the sale and financing of real estate on private and shared water wells. Well inspections should be performed by knowledgeable, licensed, and insured professionals, just like all other inspectors and consultants involved in real estate transactions. Their well inspection report should include examining and evaluating groundwater-sharing agreements for prospective buyers.

Critical Role of Groundwater-Sharing Contracts

For every person on a well-sharing agreement, only one has the well located on their land. The legal source for drinking water for all other members comes only from the written words of their sharing contract. The strength of this contract provides them with the groundwater that allows residence in their home. It should also be the document counties demand to see and evaluate before granting a Certificate of Occupancy for a new home served by a shared well.

Groundwater-sharing contracts are crucial documents that are not always given appropriate consideration by water well contractors consulting buyers considering purchase of a home on a shared well. This small but significant detail often falls through the cracks of many real estate transactions, placing some homeowners in unpleasant situations.

Analogy to Home Inspections

A close analogy to a private water well inspection is an inspection performed by a licensed home inspector. Home Inspectors have national associations to which many belong, such as ASHI® and InterNACHI®. Home inspectors are more than association-certified; a regulatory agency licenses them to perform their trade. Certification is one thing, but a license should be required to perform a consulting service to a buyer investing hundreds of thousands of dollars and many years of life in a home served by a domestic water well.

Recommendations for Licensing and Standards

To protect the health, safety, and welfare of rural home buyers, all water well inspectors for real estate sales should be licensed professionals, pre-tested for knowledge of their trade, and required to maintain continuing education to keep licenses current. They should also post a bond and carry errors and omissions (E&O) insurance as consultants. The service provided is just as crucial as those from real estate professionals, appraisers, and inspectors of homes, termites, and septic tanks—all consulting with the buyer.

Lack of Current Standards

Water well contractors currently performing domestic water well inspections lack an accepted standard of performance to compare the well against, nor a standard format to report findings. Without a standard of the trade for what a water well inspection should include and what items a water well inspector should inspect and report on, what can a home buyer assume about the validity and thoroughness of the report received today?

Essential Nature of Water Supply

Performing a water well inspection for a real estate buyer intends to assure the buyer about the most essential aspect of their new home; drinking water supply. After all, residence is possible in a home with a leaky roof, a few termites, or a slow-operating septic tank—all correctable when reported by respective inspectors. But residence is impossible in a house without good quality water at a sustainable supply.

Insurance and Liability Concerns

Performing consulting services without proper licensing and taking money from someone relying entirely on evaluation of their legal right to extract groundwater from an existing domestic water well places contractors outside coverage of general liability insurance. Water well inspectors should carry E&O insurance just as real estate professionals, home inspectors, and other professional consultants do.

Duty to Inform on Contamination

Another area of potential liability for contractors is failure to fulfill "duty to inform" the prospective buyer of potential groundwater contamination issues known in the area of the well. If a contractor failed to inform the buyer about dangers of a contaminant in the water sample not tested for levels of arsenic, uranium, TCE, or PFAS, and it was later found present, liability could arise. Further discussion of issues related to water quality sampling and testing of shared wells appears in Chapter 9 below.

Risks in Delegation and Reporting

Well-drilling contractors sending pump-installing employees to perform inspections and water quality sampling face risk. Doing so could cause the report being ruled a "negligent undertaking" if some aspect of a proper well inspection was missed or under-reported to the buyer. A water well inspection should result in a report signed by the professional who performed the inspection and bears sole responsibility for its content. Buyers pay for and expect an unbiased professional opinion about the most critical aspect of the property; good water.

Sustainability Statements and Professional Boundaries

Sustainability of future water well supply is a question frequently asked by buyers. A massive error in a well-inspection report would be statements about sustainability of groundwater resource for years to come. Making statements about groundwater's occurrence, movement, or future availability and charging for that report constitutes practicing "geology"—strictly prohibited in some states unless performed by a Registered Geologist.

Potential Conflicts of Interest

It is not unusual for water well contractors to operate as second-third, or fourth-generation family businesses. If a buyer of a shared well-supported property hires one of these family-owned contracting businesses to inspect a domestic water well drilled or equipped by their father, grandfather, or uncle, an unethical perspective could influence the report.

Alternatively, objectivity might be compromised when one contractor evaluates a shared well system drilled, constructed, and maintained by a fierce competitor. These represent reasons for advocating establishment of water well inspectors as a recognized professional trade, just as home, pest, and septic inspectors.

Call for Third-Party Professional Inspectors

Many reasons exist why the business of performing water well inspections for sale and transfer of real estate should be performed only by third-party professional water well inspectors without affiliation with a water well or pump installation company. Professional well inspectors should be vetted and tested by a regulatory agency of their state and licensed to perform this most important of all home inspections: water well consulting.

Personal Experience and Buyer Protection

As a consultant and water well inspector for prospective buyers of real estate that either supply or receive groundwater under a contract/agreement, importance was seen in clear explanation of these documents. Far too many buyers of rural property on a shared well discovered later issues with their contracts, causing problems between members challenging to resolve. Typical water well contractors lack training to evaluate shared well contracts/agreements for clients, and lawyer fees often prove too expensive for these transactions.

Having a sustainable source of potable water for a rural home remains the most critical requirement for a prospective buyer, entitling them to the best possible unbiased, competent well inspection report. Professionals should perform well inspections for sale and financing of real estate, especially when the home is on a shared well. Rural home buyers everywhere deserve it. A lifetime of happiness depends on a legally viable groundwater supply for their home, and a poorly written agreement can spoil that dream.

Chapter Nine

Water Quality Testing of Shared Groundwater Wells

Importance of Water Quality Testing in Shared Wells

Many lenders and their underwriters require some water quality testing of the water provided to borrowers. Domestic house wells lack specific water quality standards that must be met at any time over the life of the well in most states.

Most states also lack water quality standards for shared water wells. Water quality remains an essential aspect of family health that should not be taken lightly or virtually ignored, as occurs in most existing shared well agreements.

Recommended Contract Clause

Annual water quality testing should be a required clause in any groundwater-sharing contract for the safety and health of everyone in the system.

Personal perspective emphasizes reluctance to manage a shared well system without periodic testing of the water consumed daily by family and neighbors. Only a tiny percentage of well-sharing contracts require periodic water quality tests. Further, no clause has been seen stating whether the group's water quality testing information can be shared if a member wishes to sell their home to another party.

Defining "Potable" Water

The term 'potable water' represents a concept or vague understanding, not a quality standard, until universal agreement exists on tests and levels of elements or compounds meeting a standard. It often serves as a minimum requirement for acceptability for buyers. However, no single test determines what constitutes potable water.

Common Issues in Real Estate Transactions

Observation shows many sales of properties on shared wells approach closing before discovery of a lender underwriter's requirement that the water supply must be "potable". The Real Estate and Mortgage Lending industry incorrectly assumes that testing well water for presence or absence of coliform bacteria, including the secondary test for E. coli, and negative results for both, renders the water potable. This is often called the 'potability test' and is frequently requested during well inspections. The absence of bacteria in a single sample does not accurately determine that the water is safe to drink.

Sampling Confusion

Adding to confusion, the mortgage industry does not specify where to collect the water sample. Results of water quality tests can differ if collected at the wellhead or from the kitchen sink.

Groundwater from a shared well is often stored at atmospheric pressure and temperature before going to the participating homes. Poorly maintained storage tanks can impact the quality of the water delivered at the kitchen sink. Sampling water there may be more representative than sampling at the well head.

Just as ambiguous is the standard where the well inspector "certifies" that water supplied by a shared well is "safe and potable" to drink. Yet, published wording does not specify what water quality standard determines "safe" and "potable".

Figure 6 Author collecting a water sample from a kitchen sink due to lack of a sampling port at the well head.

Federal Underwriter Requirements

Mortgage Lenders often submit the following as a quality standard for water from shared systems.[9]

- Provide safe and potable water.

- An inspection is required under the same circumstances as an individual well.

This may be evidenced by:

- A letter from the health authority having jurisdiction, or

- In the absence of local health department standards, by a certified water quality analysis demonstrating that the well water complies with the Environmental Protection Agency's (EPA) National Interim Primary Drinking Water Regulations.

The EPA maintains many quality standards for drinking water in public water systems, but no water quality standards exist for private and shared water well systems in most states. However, approximately 90 maximum contaminant levels (MCLs) are specified by the EPA as standards for public water systems providing groundwater from wells.[10] The entire suite of water quality tests for a new source supply, such as a water well, can

---

[9] HUD Handbook 4000.1 pages 186-191, 479, 573, 602-604. Rev. Aug. 2023.
[10] USEPA. 2013a. National Primary and Secondary Drinking Standards. http://water.epa.gov/drink/contaminants/index. cfm Accessed 11-2013

cost $4,000 and take 30 days to process. As more contaminants are added to the EPA's list of MCLs for public water systems, some may become underwriter standards for shared wells. This standard seems impractical for small, shared water well systems to meet.

Risks for Contractors and Inspectors

In today's world, water well contractors certify shared well water meets these standards despite testing only for presence or absence of coliform bacteria. No water well contractor would want to face court action from a home buyer discovering after closing that shared water contains nitrate, arsenic, uranium, or other contaminants—or that water quality fails expected standards because it was certified as potable. The dictionary defines potable as safe to drink, aligning with common assumption of "safe to drink."

Liability Concerns

Question arises whether pump-installing contractors performing shared well inspections understand risks taken when 'certifying' water as potable based solely on coliform bacteria testing. Certifying that the water is safe to drink could be considered an implied warranty liability that the contractor has not considered.

Limitations of Lender Standards and Treatment Systems

Water quality from a shared water well could meet lender/underwriter standards and be called potable yet may not be safe enough to drink for a given homeowner.[11] In these instances, installation of a water treatment system may be needed to treat water satisfactorily. The issue then becomes whether the lending institution accepts the buyer's post-treatment water quality test in lieu of the wellhead sample.

If a homeowner relies on water treatment equipment, verification of performance as designed falls to someone. When selling the property years later, qualification of the well inspector to determine if the water treatment system remains in good working order becomes relevant.

Water well contractors performing inspections may lack training or licensing in water treatment systems, as these are different specialties—water treatment sales and servicing require a separate contractor's license in many states. For this reason, mortgage lending underwriters typically require that "well" water meet minimum standards and do not accept group or individual post-treatment sample results.

Call for State Standards and Professional Guidance

More states should adopt minimum water quality standards for both private and shared water wells that are practical and feasible to meet and protect buyers. Even minimum standards will not fully protect buyers from "forever contaminants"

---

[11] An Arizona Well Owners Guide to Water Quality and Uses. U of A Press. Jan. 2014, J. Artiola, G. Hix, et al.

measured in parts per trillion. This underscores why knowledge of potential contaminants in a given well should be part of a professional well inspector's expertise. However, state guidelines for water quality testing for buyers on private and shared wells would provide better understanding of water quality in the well-inspection report.

Chapter Ten

Performance Standards for Shared Water Wells

Figure 7 A groundwater-sharing system with a flow meter that records total usage by all members.

Lack of State Requirements and Federal Influence

Most states impose no specific requirements on the wording of contracts intended to share groundwater from domestic wells. However, certain federal mortgage underwriting agencies establish such requirements. Consequently, when a home on a shared well system enters the market, sales opportunities may be restricted to cash or conventional buyers if the share agreement wording fails to meet underwriter requirements.

VA Minimum Well Performance Requirements for Shared Wells

The following outline current minimum well performance requirements for shared well systems as defined by the VA:[12]

The Mortgagee must confirm that a shared well:

- o Serves properties that cannot feasibly connect to an acceptable public or community water supply system.
- o Provides a continuous supply of water to each involved dwelling unit, ensuring that all existing construction properties receive—at the same time—at least three gallons per minute (or five gallons per minute for proposed construction) sustained over a continuous four-hour period.
- o Demonstrates system yield through a certified pump test or other means acceptable to all agreeing parties.

---

[12] VA Pamphlet 26-7 Revised, Chapter 12 Minimum Property Requirements.

Most shared wells produce only a limited gallons-per-minute flow rate. A properly designed and constructed shared well system pumps at a sustainable rate into large storage tank(s), where a high-flowrate booster pump pressurizes a pressure tank to supply water to everyone in the system.

This VA requirement states that the well itself—not the storage tank and booster pump system—meet simultaneous demands of all homes on the system. No statement clarifies how much water defines "all domestic purposes" or the duration the well must sustain that demand. Many terms in this standard imply a warranty that the shared well system satisfies the criterion.

Challenges in Certification

As an inspector of many shared water wells, difficulty arose in certifying that the shared well under inspection met the above requirements.

- There must be a permanent easement allowing access for maintenance and repair.
- There must be a well-sharing agreement which:
- Makes reasonable and fair provisions for maintenance and repair of the system and sharing of those costs.
- Is binding on signatory parties and their successors in title.
- Is recorded in local deeds.

Practical Difficulties in Compliance

From an experienced shared well inspector, challenge exists for a well-manager of an operating system to grant permission for an inspector to conduct a pump-test of their sole source water well merely for the convenience of a prospective buyer of one share. Most shared wells remain stressed to meet demands of all members and stay productive.

Some aquifers lack capacity to constantly produce all desired water. No feasible way exists to pump-test a shared water well to waste when storage tank(s) maintain maximum capacity most of the time. Pump-testing a shared "well" to confirm it meets demand for all domestic purposes, for each member simultaneously, as required by underwriters, simply does not occur.

Call for Changes in Standards

Changes are needed to both FHA and VA standards for shared well systems so that requirements become at least practical for a well inspector to certify. As a groundwater consultant, the term "certify" means swearing and affirming that statements are correct and valid, with an obligation to stand behind the report. Professional water well inspectors would take this obligation more seriously than water well contractors.

Chapter Eleven

Useful Clauses in Groundwater-sharing Contracts

No One-Size-Fits-All Model for Groundwater-Sharing Contracts

As stated earlier, no "one model fits all" exists for creating groundwater-sharing contracts. State laws dictate some clauses as necessary while others remain optional.

Evolution of Recommended Clauses

List of clauses that should be included in any groundwater-sharing contract has evolved from what might be called "trial and error" after reviewing and evaluating hundreds of well share agreements and resolving issues that arose.

Experience in Explaining and Resolving Issues

On numerous occasions, members of a shared well received explanation of precisely what their agreement says and what it means for them. Missing clauses were pointed out along with why they caused the problem. When agreement existed amongst parties that changes were needed, explanations followed on how changes had to be made and agreed upon for implementation.

Challenges in Amending Contracts

Amendments to signed, notarized, and recorded contracts tied to real property can only occur according to the original contract's terms. If the original agreement allowed for future amendments, it should have stated required approval of a percentage of members. Often, clarity lacked on whether simple majority or unanimous approval was required.

Practical Difficulties

Unanimous approvals prove tough to obtain when a dispute over contract words has already arisen. Some buyers learned only too late that words have meaning.

Clauses that should be found in any groundwater-sharing contract

Clauses that:

1. Establish the authority granting the landowner's right to divert the groundwater to be shared.
2. Establish an intent to share the legally derived groundwater, stating if it's temporary or into perpetuity.
3. Select a name for ownership of the well site, registration of the well with state authority, contract for electrical services, name on all bank accounts, and be the named grantor on the contract to share groundwater.
4. Record the contract to share groundwater in the county where the well and land are located.

5. Place ownership of the well site property in the name of the established legal entity in the county records.

6. Word the contract agreement; as either party wall, condominium, or small business.

7. Include all the County Assessor's Parcel numbers to which the groundwater contract applies.

8. Attach a survey map locating the well(s), tanks, power supply, distribution lines, and placement of water meters.

9. Define all easements for access, water lines, and maintenance, as shown on the survey map.

10. Define the members' ability to subdivide in the future, drill their own well, and the terms for leaving the contract.

11. Define what becomes of the well and water plant if the party with the well on their land wishes to drill their own well.

12. Define what the responsibilities of a party are if they combine two lots into one lot.

13. Define allowable and non-allowable uses of water, i.e., no commercial, no crop irrigation, no filling of pools, and no excessive waste.

14. Define allocation of fees for groundwater usage monthly. Suggestion: It's best if proportional for metered water use but equal for maintenance items and outside services.

15. Define terms of office for well-manager, alternates, and treasurer, and define voting rules and member access to records.

16. Define what operational and management data will be collected and shared, when meetings will be held, and if minutes will be recorded.

17. Define penalties for late payments, loss of water service, liens on property by group, and recovery of monies.

18. Define holding and management of funds, require two signatures for checking and savings accounts, and records of deposits.

19. Define disposition of reserve funds for future maintenance and disposition of a member's share if they sell their home.

20. Define Special Assessments if needed for replacement of the well, electrical service repairs, common access roads, and water treatment.

21. Define negligence. If one party is at fault, they must pay the total cost of repairs for the issue they caused.

22. Define what water quality testing will be done and when. Who will sample, and if the results can be shared?

23. Define rationing measures to be taken in the event of an extended drought or a groundwater resource reduction mandate.

24. Define conflict resolution methods, mediation or arbitration, civil suit, and cost recovery.

25. Define the severability of one clause and the impact of that clause on any of the above clauses.

26. Define requirements for amendments and modifications if simple or super majority approval is required.

27. Define the risk of allowing others outside the defined group to get water from the system and establish a prescriptive right.

28. Define the impact on the contract if the existing well fails and drilling a new one is required.

29. Define what happens when there is a frustration or a cessation of purpose to the contract.

30. Encourage water conservation practices to protect the resource and reduce maintenance costs.

Comprehensive Nature of the Clause List

This rather extensive list may still not cover all items that could or should form part of a proper groundwater-sharing contract, but it should serve as a starting point for new contracts.

Application to Existing Agreements

For parties already bound to an existing agreement, a review against this list could identify missing elements.[13]

Risks of Incomplete Contracts

Confusion and conflict between existing agreement members become more likely due to one or more items not being included or fully defined.

---

[13] Drafting Key Provisions of a Shared Well Agreement, Arthur B. Macomber, Macomber Law PLLC. The Advocate, Idaho Water Law Section Oct. 2017.

Chapter Twelve

Lessons Learned from Past Well Share Agreements

Common Missing Clause: Funds Management (#15)

One of the most common missing clauses in older well-sharing agreements addresses who holds collected funds and how they are managed for operation and maintenance of the well (#15). The old adage that money is the root of all evil may explain why some well-sharing communities have seen operating and reserve funds disappear entirely.

Case Examples of Fund Mismanagement

One story involves a modest size shared well group where the designated well-manager, a semi-pro rodeo performer absent from home for months each year, passed responsibility for reading water meters, calculating dues, and depositing funds to his mother living with him. She kept collected funds in a bank account opened in her name. Unfortunately, the group's funds became part of her estate upon her passing.

Another larger shared well community saw husband-and-wife managers disappear entirely (leaving the country), taking approximately twenty-thousand dollars with them. This occurred because funds were held in a bank account requiring only one signature for dispersal (his). This burdened each community member with meeting electrical service and minor maintenance fees until reserve funds could rebuild.

Disputes Over Ownership Claims

Records contain many instances of shared well owners reporting that one group member falsely claimed ownership of the shared well system, even if the well was not located on their land. Numerous ruses have supported false ownership claims, demanding a clause that clearly defines ownership of the groundwater being shared in the contract.

Recommended Supporting Elements

These statements should follow with a map illustrating all parcels of land included in the contract, location of the well to be shared, outlines of easements for utilities, and local assessor parcel numbers. This eliminates disputes over intended shares in the contract.

Unauthorized Membership and Related Clauses (#6–#9)

One situation escalated to members pointing guns at each other after one member granted unauthorized membership to a friend, contrary to the agreement. This settled before a judge. This exemplifies the importance of clauses like numbers #6 to #9 in the essential clauses list.

Issues with Oversized Groups

Another case highlighted risks when a shared well group grows too large. Members complained that the well manager constantly raised fees without input. Rates increased in stages for metered customers while broken-meter members paid a minimum flat rate. Discovery revealed thirty-seven active members on a fifty-lot agreement, classifying it as a non-compliant public water system under local environmental authority. Members then faced costs to achieve compliance with the local health authority.

Non-Residential Applications

Contracts for sharing groundwater extend beyond single-family residences. One opportunity involved conducting an inspection and preparing a report to resolve conflict between two wine growers overuse or misuse of a shared well. It was headed to court until realization that court costs exceeded mediated resolution costs. This often occurs with shared well disagreements—resolving differences rarely justifies attorney fees and court costs. Best practice constructs the groundwater-sharing contract correctly from the start.

Advocacy for Small Business Model (Type C, #3)

These represent reasons for often recommending the small business model (Type C) for proper groundwater-sharing contracts. With clauses structured this way (#3), requiring a registered name for the well-sharing group, a business bank account in the same name, and designated responsibility for electrical service operating the well and booster equipment, groups face far less risk of similar fates. A two-signature requirement for checking and possible savings accounts assures members that funds remain available for significant maintenance expenses.

Clauses indexed as #5 and #8 strongly indicate preference for structuring agreements so that the well, storage tanks, booster pump, pressure tanks, electrical service, and control equipment locate on a parcel belonging to the small business model's established name. A detailed drawing of all parcels involved and dedicated easements for utilities should accompany this structure.

Consequences of Fragmented Ownership

Failure to adhere to this policy caused tremendous troubles and expenses for years in a sixteen-lot shared well agreement. Known as the Two Tanks Well Share Co-Op, the well resided on one member's property, two storage tanks on another's, and the power pedestal on a third's land. Disputes escalated when the landowner with the power pedestal claimed ownership and attempted takeover of the entire system.

The absence of clearly worded clauses placing all components on a single parcel, preferably in the small business's name, fueled a ten-year dispute. The full story appears in Arizona court record,[14] plus various local news stories about members' plight. Repeated transfers of well registration between parties prompted requirements for proof of land ownership for legal groundwater extraction. This case reinforced the necessity of clearly defining all parcels, especially the well parcel, in contract wording and maps.

Cost Allocation Friction (#11)

Probably the most common source of friction among shared well members arises from allocating costs (#11). No one wants to pay for unreceived benefits or others' water usage. Nevertheless, agreements abound where each homeowner pays the same monthly amount regardless of individual usage. This form of cost-sharing becomes necessary if members lack individual metering, a major oversight by small-time developers during original system construction.

Benefits of Metering

Lack of individual water meters has led to numerous disputes. Properly prepared contracts include explicit wording mandating a separate power meter for the water plant, a water meter on the well, and individual water meters for each member. With these in place, more equitable and accurate cost allocation

---

[14] Two Tanks v. Rosas Water Co. Maricopa County Superior Court. 2016.

maintains. Additional benefits include locating system leaks or single-member misuse.

Responsibility for Negligence or Malice (#18)

If one member causes hardship or unusual expenses due to negligence or malicious intent, that member—and not others— should assume responsibility and pay the extra expense (#18). When agreement wording includes this arrangement, it typically designates one well-owner association member as responsible for monthly meter reading, generating individual bills, and enforcing rules for everyone's benefit.

Figure 8 A bank of water meters, each with an isolation valve, located at the shared well site for ease of collecting monthly readings.

Chapter Thirteen

Something for Shared Well Managers

Prevalence and Management of Shared Water Wells

As stated above, shared water wells serving two or more households represent a way of life throughout much of the US. However, very few references exist regarding daily management and use of them. Most current shared well managers remain unaware that very few laws, rules, and regulations govern their drinking water supply. Purpose of Chapter 13 of this Revised Edition 2026 serves as a reference guide for shared well managers—and others—who need more information about shared water wells.

Typically, shared well managers are volunteers drafted into the position out of necessity or property ownership. They must now serve and protect a group of homeowners who are dependent on groundwater from a single domestic water well. It has proved a thankless and daunting task in some situations.

Chapter Objectives

The purpose of this chapter outlines the kinds of issues volunteer well managers might face and provides guidance on how to deal with them.

Shared Well Management - *Wells and Public Water Systems*

Figure 9 An example of a fenced, equipped and nicely maintained shared well system.

The federal definition of a public water system under the Safe Drinking Water Act includes systems with at least 15 service connections or that regularly serve an average of at least 25 individuals for at least 60 days out of the year.

Many shared well systems operate today serving fewer than 15 homes but with more than 25 full-time residents (due to larger households). A very thin line exists between a private shared well system and a public water system. Managers must determine with certainty which category their system falls into—often by counting service connections and estimating average daily number of persons being served.

Regulatory Implications

Systems meeting the public water system criteria qualify as such technically and face a different set of rules for operation and management. Public systems often fall under regulation by county offices or Departments of Environmental Quality.

However, minimal information exists from any governmental agency about managing private shared water well systems.

Purpose of This Section

This section for well managers covers current standard procedures and practices pertaining to managing shared wells, along with additional related issues.[15]

---

[15] A Guide for Operating Shared Water Wells in Arizona, U of A Coop Ext.   Bulletin 1810, Feb 2020. G. Hix, et al.

A Checklist of Things Shared Well Managers Should Do

Step One: Registration and Pump Installation Form

The first priority for a shared well manager involves confirming proper registration of the well under state jurisdiction in the name of either:

- The owner of the land upon which the well is located, or a properly designated and licensed operator of the well.

Preferably, shared wells register in the name of a well Association, Co-Op, or Limited Liability Company. When the shared water well is located on a manager's private land, steps should transfer responsibility for the well out of that person's name.

An equally important task documents the size of pump and motor installed in the well, static and pumping water levels, and confirms the flow rate with a four-hour pump test. A shared well manager should maintain a written record of the make, model and performance of the equipment in the well and its setting depth. Additionally, records should be kept to the non-pumping and pumping water levels as measured in the well.

Forms are available to preserve the most relevant information about the well. This important information belongs in any shared well manager's notebook along with copies of each item listed below.

Step Two: Verify the Number of People Being Served

The second priority verifies the number of connections to the system and how many people live in each home. If the count of persons relying on the system exceeds twenty-five, contact occurs with the local county Department of Environmental Quality to report this. Self-reporting as an unreported public water supply proves better than discovery by authorities enforcing regulations with little grace.

A well share manager's notebook contains names, addresses, phone numbers, emails, etc., of each person receiving water from the well. A copy of this list resides with an alternate manager for emergencies or when the primary well manager is unavailable.

Step Three: Test Water Quality

Sampling and testing of water quality served by the well represents a critical responsibility. Clean, safe, potable water constitutes an essential element for any home when public water supply is unavailable. The source and quality of water for a home hold equal—or perhaps greater—importance compared to a good roof or working air conditioner. The single most important asset to any home is water, and that source may come from a shared water well.

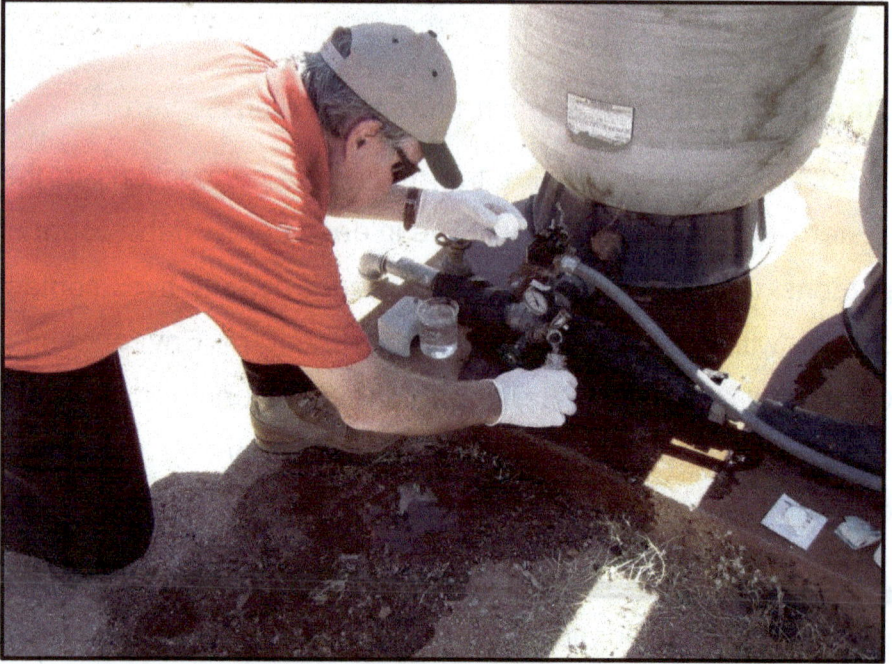

Figure 10 Author collecting a water sample from a shared water well system just before it enters two bladder tanks.

Absence of Regulatory Standards

No laws, regulations, or standards exist in most states governing what people consume from private or shared wells. Still, no shared well manager would want to explain delivery of poor quality or contaminated water to neighboring users. Periodic water quality testing may not be legally required for shared wells, but it remains the right action for a well manager.

Recommended Testing Schedule

At minimum, shared wells should undergo checking twice a year for presence of coliform bacteria and once a year for nitrite, total dissolved solids, and pH. Testing every three to five years should cover arsenic, uranium, mercury, and fluoride. Additional tests may apply in areas known for man-made contaminants.[16]

No sensible person would want designation as manager of a private water system without regular water quality monitoring. Yet many shared well managers likely neglect this vital function.

Potential Liability

Could such a manager face consideration as negligent for failing to protect well-share members' health through periodic testing? If the well share agreement requires periodic water-quality testing, compliance becomes essential.

Growing Importance for Homebuyers

Water quality is of increasing concern to today's homebuyers. Media stories have highlighted horrible consequences of contaminated water consumption, raising awareness. Buyers seek assurance of good quality water. However, no stated water-quality standards exist for private or shared water-well systems. Few state or county agencies specifically oversee or

---

[16] An Arizona Well Owners Guide to Water Quality and Uses. U of A Press, Jan. 2014. J. Artiola, G. Hix, et al.

regulate water quality from private and shared wells. Thus, responsibility falls to the well manager to protect everyone's health through testing.

Disclosure Requirements in Sales

When a family attempts purchase of an existing property served by a private or shared well, the seller must complete and present information about the legal water source. Disclosure of any known past or present water quality issues is required. If on a shared well, the seller may consult the well manager for necessary information to complete the disclosure form. A shared well manager should maintain basic information in a file, available to any member selling or refinancing their home—unless prohibited by agreement wording.

Laboratory Testing Process

Water-quality testing laboratories willingly test well water for requested parameters. However, they do not interpret results regarding potential adverse health effects from reported concentration levels. Certified laboratory procedures can require seven to twelve working days for sample preparation, testing, documentation for quality assurance and accuracy, and report delivery.

Costs for periodic sampling and testing of everyone's water quality should be shared equally among all members of the shared well system.

Future Concerns and Record-Keeping

These represent triggers to issues rarely covered elsewhere. Importance of these issues will grow as drinking water quality becomes everyone's greatest health concern. At minimum, a well manager should maintain water quality information on file and make it available to all well share owners, mirroring requirements placed on public water systems managers.

Figure 11 A shared well system with a storage tank and a hydro-pneumatic pressure tank, but no fence.

Step Four: Well Performance Records

Verification and documentation of the well's performance and productivity represent key responsibilities. The most common productivity for a shared well likely falls below fifteen gallons per minute. However, the well's productivity in gallons per minute (GPM) matters less than the total gallons per day it can produce.

A well producing as little as five GPM can still serve several homes. Low-productivity wells incorporate storage tanks to hold large quantities of water at atmospheric temperature and pressure until needed. Booster pumps then provide flow and pressure to meet system demands.

Water demands typically peak twice daily—once in the morning and again in the evening—for an hour or two each time. The delivery system must handle these peak demands while maintaining adequate pressure. The well replenishes storage drawdown between peaks. This explains why total daily gallons producible by the well far outweigh the pump's GPM rate.

Essential Records for Managers

A shared well manager should maintain accurate, permanent records covering:

- Well performance
- Booster pump operation
- System pressure regulation
- Power consumption
- Water quality test results
- Operational expenses
- Water table measurements

In some well share groups, the well manager and treasurer serve as separate roles. Financial health concerns everyone, so financial records require careful, accurate maintenance and availability to all members.

Buyer Protections and Manager Awareness

Buyers of real estate on shared water wells receive no protection or warranty from state agencies regarding water rights, proper well construction, pumping equipment condition, or water quality. Only limited counties enforce local or national plumbing and electrical codes on shared wells. This creates a strict "buyer beware" situation, and all shared well managers should recognize this.

Tracking Equipment Performance

Records should document performance of the well and pumping equipment, illustrating functionality. Measurement of gallons per kilowatt hour can reveal declining well performance over time, as illustrated in Figure 12 below.

A slow decline in gallons per kilowatt hour signals the well manager when pump and motor replacement become necessary.[17]

---

[17] Hard data collected and graphed by a shared well manager that indicated it was time to install a new pump in the well. Personal communication.

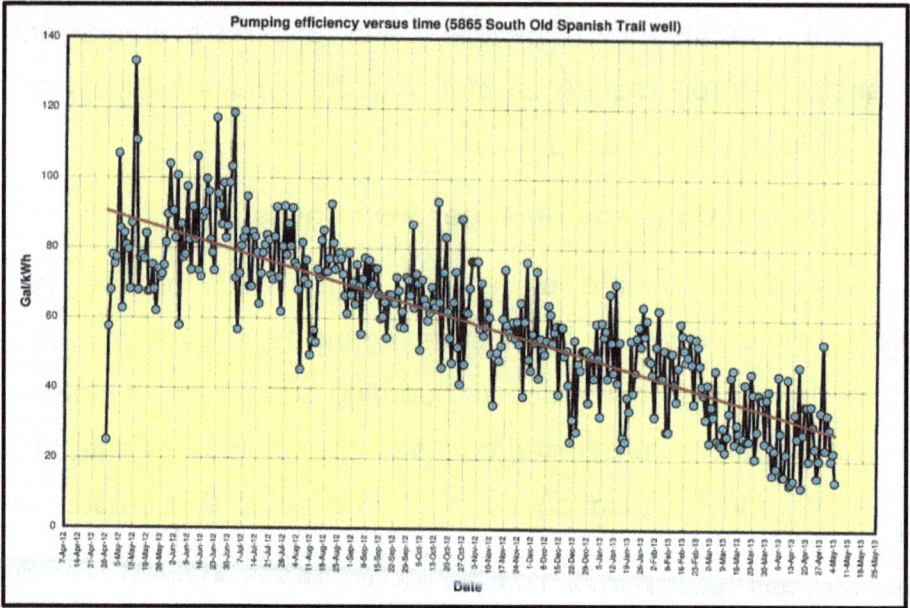

Figure 12 Example of how monitoring gallons pumped per kilowatt hour of electricity used over time will show a declining efficiency.

Evaluating System Efficiency

Water well and water plant performance evaluates best through periodic (weekly, monthly, yearly) efficiency—gallons pumped or distributed per energy required (gallons per kilowatt hour). Often termed the water-to-wire ratio, this bottom-line metric requires tracking by shared well managers. Calculation demands dedicated water and electrical meters for the system.

If the shared well system uses a single power meter for the well and two booster pumps, a separate hour meter can log well run time, separable from the total power bill. This enables water-to-wire efficiency calculation for the well and booster(s).

Comprehensive Documentation

A prudent well manager creates or maintains a complete paper file including:

- Water well driller's report
- Pump installation information
- Water level measurements
- Well performance in GPM, gallons per day, week, or month
- Monitoring power consumption for all system equipment proves essential for monthly charge distribution.

Step Five: System Design & As Built Drawings

Security and Access to the Well Site

A shared well site should remain fenced and padlocked at all times. Access to the well, storage tank(s), booster pumps, and pressure vessels should restrict to the well manager, the designated water plant operator (if a public supply system), and water well contractors. Provision should include a smaller person-access gate and a larger dual gate for vehicle access to the well head.

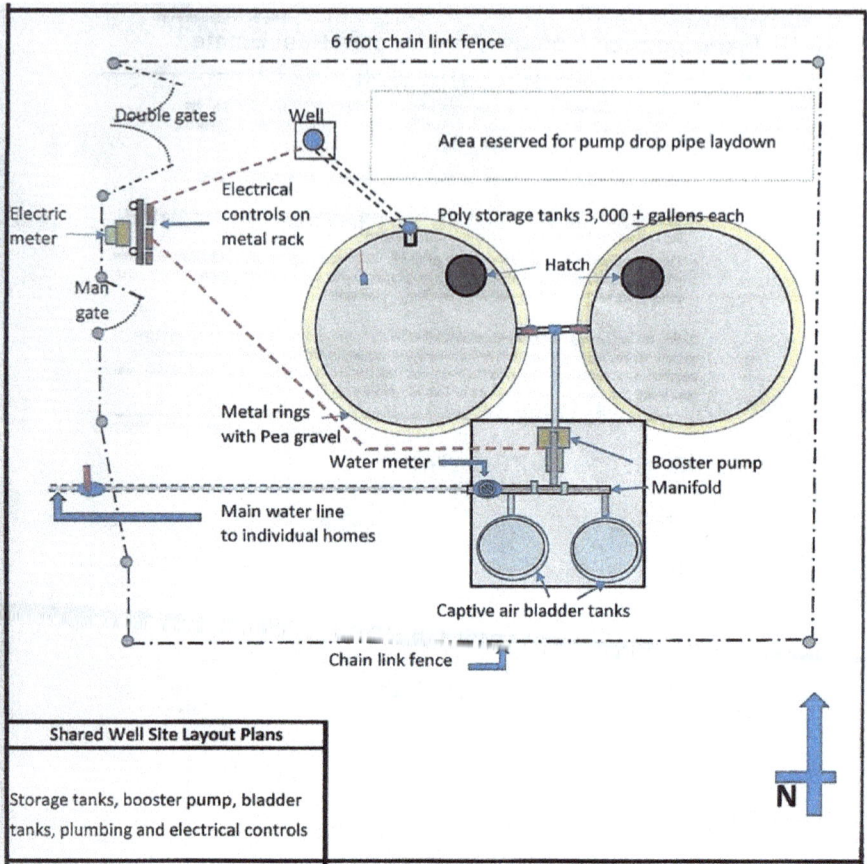

Figure 13 An example of a site plan for a groundwater-sharing system.

Considerations for Buildings Around Wells

Well managers sometimes construct small buildings containing the well and associated equipment, assuming better protection for the system. While potentially more secure, this approach complicates pump replacement. Pulling a well pump requires a medium-size truck and pump hoist to back up within five to eight feet of the well head for removing pump in twenty- or twenty-one-foot pipe lengths and laying them down. This task becomes more difficult and dangerous for the crew if the well locates inside a building or behind a block wall.

Properly constructed and plumbed water wells require no building enclosure for protection from elements. Shared wells can utilize pitless adapters to keep all electrical and plumbing underground, away from elements. Figure 14 below illustrates a well equipped with a pitless adapter. This connection method eliminates need for building enclosure. Attachment 1 at the end of the book provides a drawing of a typical pitless-adapted well equipped with a pump.

Figure 14 A pitless adapter well serving a summer home community is impervious to weather conditions and is easily accessible for maintenance.

Individual Valves and Meters

Individual distribution valves for each member on the shared well system prove almost necessary. If the agreement language specifies the authority to shut-off of a person's water supply for non-payment of regular water use share or special assessments for repairs, the well manager **must** ensure compliance. Individual supply line valves and water meters become essential for identifying which member's line may have a leak. Even small leaks affect everyone on the system.

Protection of Above-Ground Plumbing

Above-ground plumbing to and from booster pumps typically requires wrapping with insulating foam and metallic tape for protection from penetrating summer sun rays and cold winter temperatures. Individual wrapping of above-ground plumbing recommends over covering with blankets for several reasons. Covering well equipment with blankets, tarps, rugs, etc., attracts rodents—and where rodents appear, reptiles that feed on them likely follow. Neither proves desirable near a potable water system. Rodents leave droppings potentially containing E. coli bacteria, and certain reptiles and insects can harm well managers when suddenly uncovered.

Maintenance of Site Appearance

The shared well site represents a valuable component of everyone's drinking water source. It should always appear clean, secure, and sanitary. This vitally important asset supports homes, families, and neighbors. It should never serve as storage for broken equipment or become overgrown with weeds. If serving as well manager, responsibility includes ensuring the site remains a model of cleanliness for those dependent on it.

Mechanical Issues

Helpful Hints for Situations Well Managers May Encounter

No Water Calls

One member reports no water at their home. The first action for a well manager determines if the same condition exists at their own home. If yes, it likely affects everyone else as well. This requires a trip to the well site regardless of time of day or night.

Diagnosis at the Site

Once at the site, determination focuses on whether the issue lies with the well or the booster pump. If the shared well pumps to an above-ground storage tank, it needs at least two-thirds full for operation. Less than one-third full may indicate the booster pump halts due to extremely low water level. This points to the well not working.

A shared well manager should check for tripped circuit breakers or blown fuses related to the well and prepare to cycle breakers or test/replace fuses.

Advanced Checks

One additional test an experienced well manager can perform verifies the problem resides with the well before calling a service contractor.

Overload protection devices typically monitor submersible pump motors and allow reset if the condition proves intermittent or signals impending failure without complete breakdown. Managers should gain sufficient knowledge of location and operation of these resettable overload or under-load devices for reading or resetting.

Low Storage Scenarios

The well may have stopped sufficiently long ago for significant storage tank drawdown triggering the low liquid level switch to prevent booster pump operation and total tank emptying. This scenario occurs with both above-ground and in-ground storage tanks.

Some above-ground storage tanks feature a sliding target on the side providing constant visual indication of internal water levels. In-ground storage tank can be equipped with alarm systems that alert the well manager when the water level reaches a set limit.

Benefits of Accurate Diagnosis

Proper diagnosis by the well manager of the likely problem area before contacting the service contractor assists tremendously and potentially saves significant time in obtaining correct repair parts. Informing the service contractor of current pump size and horsepower proves especially helpful. Availability of well records for this purpose accelerates system restoration to operation.

Helpful Hints for Situations Well Managers May Encounter

Low Pressure at Some Homes

When the water system operates normally but one or more customers complain of persistently low water pressure—or low pressure only at certain times—this represents a common issue. Most shared well systems maintain on-off operating pressure between 40 and 60 PSI or 50 to 70 PSI. The twenty-pound differential aligns with settings common to most manufacturers' pressure switches.

These pressure switch range settings can adjust manually upward or downward to meet system demands. However, changing the pressure switch setting also requires adjusting the pre-charge in captive air bladder tanks, if used. See bladder tank manufacturer's recommended pre-charge pressure settings for proper operation.

Types of Pressure Tanks

Two styles of pressure tanks commonly serve shared well systems.

Hydro-Pneumatic Tanks (Older Style)

The older style, called a hydro-pneumatic tank, allows direct contact between air and water inside the tank. Water does not compress, so air compresses as water forces into the tank, and compressed air pushes water out when drawn from the plumbing system. These typically appear as long horizontal steel tanks on support legs holding 500 to 1,000 gallons of water.

Captive Air Bladder Tanks (Modern Style)

The other common style uses a bank of two or more captive air bladder tanks with a bladder or diaphragm separating water from compressing air. These tanks require pre-charge pressure set to just two pounds less than the "come on" setting of the pressure switch.

Overcharging or undercharging bladders or diaphragms quickly shortens their lifespan. Adjusting pressure switch settings proves best performed by a well service contractor if the well manager lacks familiarity with these procedures.

- Causes of Pressure Loss
- Water distribution lines lose pressure due to:

- Distance from the pressurizing source
- Elevation increases

Number Of Bends and Reductions in Pipe Sizes

Additionally, parties on the far end of dead-end water supply lines notice pressure drops when closer parties draw water. For this reason, the well manager should have an accurate as-built drawing of the well location, all equipment on the well site, the location of water delivery lines and water meter locations to each member's property line. There should also be an as-built drawing clearly indicating all easements for access and egress to the well site and for all water delivery lines to all parcels. There should also be an easement of record for contactor access to the well site.

Solutions for Affected Members

Shared well systems that have groundwater wells that produce limited flow rates may not be able to meet peak demands for all members at all times. If the single source groundwater well fails and must be replaced, all members can be without water.

For these cases, each member might install their own smaller water storage tank with a personal booster pump and bladder tank. This provides an advantage over other system designs. If the shared well or booster pump fails, they can maintain their own water supply. With their own storage tank and booster system they can also purchase water and have it delivered.

Sudden Increases in Water Use

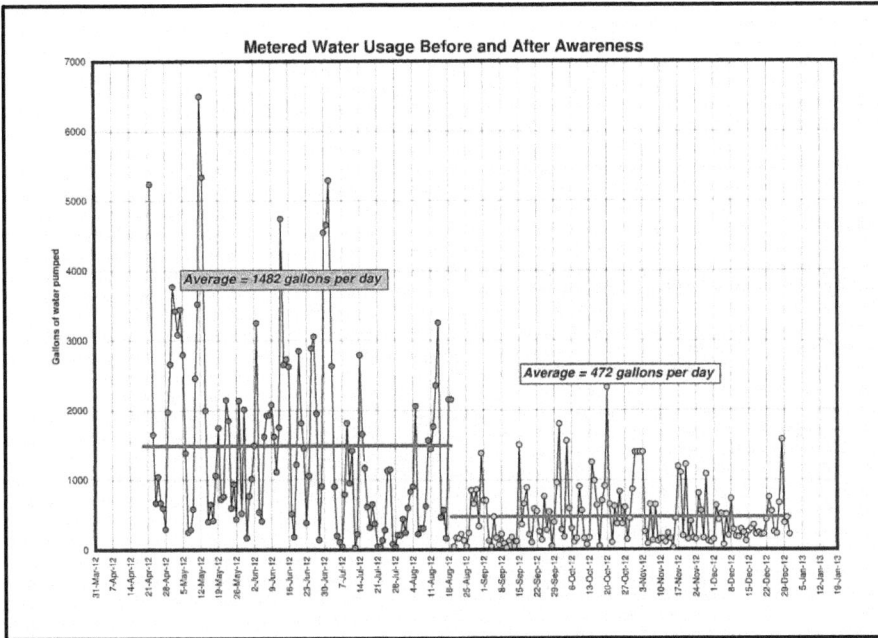

Figure15 Graph shows the effect of reporting water system consumption to shared well members. Personal communication.

Sharp increases in water use by one or more members can strain both mechanical aspects of the system and interpersonal relationships among members. Shared well systems structured for equal monthly or billing cycle payments face particular frustration when certain individuals use far more than average yet pay only the same amount for use and maintenance.

This represents one reason why individually metered services with proportional rates—rather than equal amounts—should be implemented. Individual water meters immediately reveal where water has gone.

Reporting total group water use or individual member consumption each month helps keep usage reasonable.

Once the well manager began reporting individual consumption, dramatic reduction in overall use occurred. No member wanted designation as the biggest water user on the system.

Finding a Reliable Well Service Contractor

Shared well managers should exclusively use services of local licensed water well and pump contractors. Handyman contractors typically lack licensing as water well contractors, potentially violating contracting laws. They may also lack full experience with a complex water well system.

Additionally, they likely lack contractor's liability insurance to protect the well group in cases of dropped pumps or catastrophic on-site accidents. Well managers should always engage licensed professional water well contractors.

Unforeseen Major Expenses

Wells can fail or collapse, and storage tanks can rust out, requiring major unplanned or unbudgeted expenses. One common failure involves complex distinction between natural occurrence and actions by well-intentioned individuals.

Many times, a well pump fails, prompting a call to a well service contractor for investigation and repairs. An experienced and licensed water well contractor diagnoses potential cause of pump and motor failure before pulling the pump. If diagnosis correctly determines need for pump removal for repair or replacement, complications can arise. Sometimes during pump pulling, the well casing attempts to rise or the pump sticks and refuses removal.

This unforeseen condition creates difficulty for both the water well contractor and well share group. If the contractor cannot diagnose and demonstrate the problem prior to pulling attempt and fails to advise the well manager of existing serious well issues, it may appear the contractor caused the problem. Truth more likely indicates that continued motor operation without water movement overheated water in the pump, melting PVC well casing and/or drop pipe. The pump and motor may have already failed for unknown reasons and compromised the well before the contractor arrived.

Common Well Failure Causes

Many modern domestic water wells drill and case with 4½-, 5-, and 5½-inch inside diameter PVC casings. Most submersible pumps and motors measure 4 inches in diameter, creating tight fit. Pumps become stuck in PVC casings due to sediment entering through casing openings above pump depth setting, trapping it. Other times, heat from pump and motor operation without cooling water flow melts PVC casing around pump and motor. In other wells, calcium carbonate buildup from precipitates in the groundwater plugs the pump or galvanic corrosion causes pump detachment from the drop pipe.

If pump, motor, drop pipe, and copper wire submersible cable cannot be retrieved (fished out), the well may be ruined, necessitating new drilling. Since well drilling contractors cannot drill through PVC, copper wire, and stainless-steel motors, a new location is required. The distance to a new location incurs additional expenses for relocating electrical and plumbing back to the original well site and water distribution lines.

People Issues

Unauthorized Access and Tampering

Shared wells and associated tanks, booster pumps, and electrical controls should always locate inside secured access fenced enclosure. All equipment associated with shared wells constitutes at least an attractive nuisance or invitation to trespassing and tampering with drinking water. For protection of drinking water alone, access should be secure with only authorized persons permitted entry.

Even recognized well share group members should prohibit entry to water plant compound without authorization. Members have attempted changes or repairs to connected systems, causing additional equipment damage. Designation of well manager and alternate manager with gate keys should be standard for properly managed systems.

Late or Non-Payment Users

Dealing with slow or late payments by specific members represents a common well managers headache. Manager ability to address late and non-payment is largely controlled by well share agreement wording. A specific clause stating individual water shut-off valves are to be used for dealing with late or non-payment must be clearly stated in the document for legal execution.

Turning off someone's water for late or non-payment may prove illegal absent explicit authorizing words in the agreement.

Excessive or Unauthorized Use of Water

No two homes use exactly same water amount, even with identical home and lot sizes. Homes occupy by varying numbers of people with different habits and needs. Some prove careless, leaving water running.

Some shared well share group's structure their water rates in a tiered scale: first 5,000 gallons per month at one cost, next 2,500 at increased per-gallon rate, over 10,000 at even higher rato. Tiered pricing and reporting individual use to all members applies peer pressure, prompting many to reduce usage. Fairness demands avoidance of one customer using 30% of total pumped water while paying only 15% of billed usage.

Unauthorized uses include domestic well water for commercial purposes or bypassing meter. Instances document well share members stealing water from own group. Individual water meters and isolation valves per home help manage agreement violations.

Negligence Causing Extra Expenses

Some well share agreements contain clause stating that if one member's negligence and excessive use cause system damage, they alone bear repair costs. This provision nearly mandates individual monthly-read water meters. Adjacent to each meter a valve should place allowing isolation of leaking systems without affecting other users.

Excessive leakage or usage by one party causing damage to well or shared equipment should bear sole cost, not equal division. Leaving irrigation hose running, drawing down water and damaging pump or draining storage tank and damaging booster pump, occurs commonly. Other members should not pay for repairs caused by one person's negligence.

Amending or Modifying an Existing Agreement

Often desirable to change existing agreement for improvements or better management. Recorded agreements represent legal contracts between two or more parties tied to real estate. Besides individual landowner interests, mortgage lenders hold vested interest in water source for home financing. Changes to properly executed and recorded agreements occur only under original document terms and conditions.

If original agreement required unanimous party agreement for changes, task proves far more difficult than simple majority stipulation. This refers not to original signers but current successors and assigns with interest in well. If original document clearly allowed simple majority changes, modifications ease. Amended agreement must reference original, stating it modifies and amends. Often, original and amended agreements record simultaneously in county where well locates.

A good agreement sets procedures for calling and holding regular and emergency meetings among members. Regularly scheduled meetings allow expression of views and resolution of issues surrounding billing procedures and planned/unplanned repairs. Financial statement review should occur then. Emergency meetings may be necessary in case of a sudden unexpected expense or water outages.

Chapter Fourteen

What the Future Holds for Shared Well Users

Figure 16 A shared well system may not always provide sufficient water for everyone using it.

Lack of an Assured Supply

Most shared water-well systems operate with little or no legal claim to adequate water services into the future. The well-share document typically provided to buyers during transfer of a vacant lot may create impression of perpetual adequate water service. Unfortunately, this proves not always true.

One reason for this situation stems from efforts to meet demand for new homes at affordable prices. Five- to ten-acre parcels legally divided into several smaller lots. Subsequent division created new property owners expecting water delivery from the Well Owners Association. Thus, the Well Share Agreement should address rights and responsibilities of subsequent landowners. Even more importantly, members should seriously consider whether the well—or more correctly, the aquifer from which water draws—can support future demands.

When constructing original well-share agreements, most developers stated that the agreement created no explicit or implied warranty as to well productivity or water quality from the aquifer. As developments reach built-out condition, last members to build homes discover system inability to support additional demands. What functioned well for initial homeowners often falls short of collective needs. More well shares authorized than system or aquifer could support. Some shortages resolve with additional equipment like larger storage tanks and booster pumps; others cannot.

Original water-system equipment likely purchased based solely on lowest bidder criterion. Hence, mechanical system meets only fraction of total peak demand for all shareholders. Mechanical parts may never have been engineered to handle peak demands. Almost certainly, aquifer never fully evaluated for sustained demands of mini-development. Most jurisdictions do not require small developers prove aquifer capability to support total future collective homeowner demand.

Guaranteed Rights to Water Service

What guaranteed rights to water service do individual lot owners under any well-share agreement hold? The most accurate answer: none. This question is rarely considered during prospective purchaser review of a well-share agreement. Therefore, shared well managers should encourage everyone on the system to appreciate and conserve water to maximum extent.

Fewer Options in the Future

Countless Well Owners Associations will find drilling existing well deeper not viable. Many wells drilled for these small developments cased with 4 ½ and 5 in diameter PVC casing; most modern well-drill pipe measures four and a half inches outside diameter and cannot fit inside these casings. Many existing shared wells cannot be deepened, new boreholes must be drilled and new wells constructed.

Another potential problem arises if original well-share document allocated only thirty-foot-by-thirty-foot well site for original water well and related equipment. No room remains on original site for replacement well drilling. When drafting original well-share agreements, developers failed to anticipate the space needed for well-drilling equipment twenty to fifty years later.

This hidden problem originated in the past and deferred to present and future well-share owners.

Figure 17: A modern drill rig drilling a domestic water well needs sufficient room to operate.

Another reason deeper drilling may not solve ultimate peak water demands could prove geologic. Not all aquifers extend deeper than original drilling depth. The specific well location determines potential for more water at greater depth. In the not-so-distant future, numerous associations will face few or no options to maintain a sufficient groundwater supply. Expense of new or replenishment water source likely triggers claims against developers and builders of these systems. However, the developer will long be gone.

Summary

Advocate For Future Groundwater-Sharing

Figure 18 Groundwater-sharing in its most basic form. Source of photo unknown.

Well Share Agreements will persist for some time, but they should transition from the past and be replaced with Groundwater-Sharing Contracts, as that accurately reflects the intent of all parties involved. Parties seek to share the legally extracted, naturally occurring resource—groundwater—fairly and proportionally under a legal contract that serves home needs with a reliable, sustainable source of proven quality drinking water.

Home buyers on shared well systems deserve precise knowledge of what they acquire or enter into. Lending institutions require assurance that funded homes maintain a viable water source, at least until loan repayment. Lending underwriters need information to ensure shared well standards remain practical for professional well inspectors to certify. Water well inspections for buyers should perform only by licensed professionals capable of evaluating a groundwater-sharing contract.

Groundwater-Sharing Contracts dedicates to introducing the concept of groundwater-sharing for the future. Titles of other helpful resources appear in the Resources and Reference Section below.

Glossary

Absolute dominion: One of five basic water law concepts some states use as the basis for ownership and groundwater use.

Certify; certified: A true and exact copy of the original or a testimonial that either the person, the process, or the report are purported to be true, accurate, and meet the standards of that certifying body.

Coliform: Coliform bacteria are organisms in the environment and in the feces of all warm-blooded animals, including humans. Detecting coliform bacteria in drinking water indicates that disease-causing organisms (pathogens) could be in the water system.

Consultant: An individual with specific knowledge and skills on a subject who, typically, is licensed or certified to advise others with less knowledge of the subject.

Contractors: A person or a business entity licensed by a state or lesser authority to perform a specific trade of providing services and products to customers for compensation.

Correlative rights doctrine: One of the five fundamental concepts of water law used by some states as the basis for ownership and use of groundwater.

Domestic well (exempt well): Wells used for single-family residences (also shared wells) are exempt from reporting water pumping or meeting water quality standards. Exempt well owners are responsible for assuring their water is safe to drink.

Easements: A granted non-possessory property right to use some aspect of another person's property, often defined as temporary or in perpetuity. Easements can be used in sharing agreements for the placement of the water lines from the well site to individual homes.

Exempt Wells: Sixteen states currently utilize the term "exempt wells" to refer to wells of "de-minimus" withdrawal or consumption of groundwater. In most states, exempt wells are not required to be metered, report annual pumpage, or have any minimum water quality standards. Utah is the only state where all private water wells must have a state-granted water right.

Gallons per minute (GPM): Gallons per minute is an instantaneous measurement (one-minute interval) of the flow rate of water from a well, produced by that pump. It may or may not be an accurate value of the long-term sustainable pumping rate of the well or the aquifer. A measurement of gallons per day (GPD) that the well can produce would be a better method to compare and classify the productivity of a given well.

Geology: The science of studying the elements and structure of planetary bodies like the earth, moon, Mars, etc. It includes the study of the occurrences, usage, and natural movement of groundwater.

FHA: Federal Housing Administration. The US Department of Housing and Urban Development that provides housing insurance on home loans.

Groundwater: Hydrogeologists define groundwater as water below the ground's surface that is saturated and not part of a definite channel or cavern (as in karst topography), filling the interstitial space around sands and gravels. It is also defined as the naturally occurring water-filling cracks and fractures in consolidated rocks. Most states consider groundwater a naturally occurring resource that belongs to the citizens of that state until legally captured.

Hauled-water homes: Hauled-water homes are homes that are not connected to a city water source or have a private domestic water well. These properties have a cistern or a large water tank that services the home's needs. This tank needs filling regularly, depending upon the water-use habits of the occupants. Some homeowners haul their water themselves; others have it delivered until they can obtain water from a private or shared water well.

HUD: Housing and Urban Development. Federal Governmental Agency that assists people seeking home loans.

Implied warranty: A verbal statement or the wording in a contract that implies that something will be good and serviceable or that a resource will be provided for some time.

Irrigation well: Irrigation wells are non-exempt and used for commercial agriculture. Irrigation wells typically have a pumping capacity greater than domestic wells, and in most states, they have to report their groundwater pumping totals at least annually for regulatory management, taxation, or both.

Limited liability company (LLC): Like a corporation, a limited liability company, or LLC, is a separate and distinct legal entity. This means an LLC can get a tax-identification number, open a bank account, and do business, all under its own name. One of the primary advantages of an LLC is that its owners, called members, have limited liability, meaning that, under most circumstances, they are not personally liable for the debts and liabilities of the LLC.

Maximum contaminate level (MCL): The Environmental Protection Agency (EPA) has established a rather lengthy list of natural and anthropogenetic elements and compounds that cannot be present in public water supplies greater than their established limit.

Non-exempt: A non-exempt well must report the volume pumped (irrigation, industrial, and municipal wells) and monitor and report water quality for drinking water purposes (municipal wells and some industrial wells).

Terminology used in states where there are exempt wells:

- **Prior appropriation doctrine:** One of five basic water law concepts some states use as the basis for ownership and groundwater use.

- **Restatement of torts rule:** One of five basic water law concepts some states use as the basis for ownership and groundwater use.

- **Reasonable use rule:** One of five basic water law concepts some states use as the basis for ownership and groundwater use.

Subsidence: When appreciable amounts of groundwater have been pumped from a specific aquifer, generally greater that 150-feet of water table decline, the overburden soil compacts to fill the support once filled by groundwater gravity pulls the surface downward.

Sustained yield: Sustained yield of a water well is the flow rate that does not cause continued drawdown of the water level in the well. Extraction rate equals recharge rate for the normal pumping cycle.

VA: Veterans Administration. Providing services to active and retired members of the military.

About the Author

Readers might ask, "What makes you an expert on Well Share Agreements?" A reply would acknowledge the question and pose a counter: "What defines an expert on groundwater-sharing? Are there accepted credentials for such an expert? Doubt exists that any will be found, but credentials and experiences can be presented for qualifications to write about groundwater-sharing contracts."

Credentials and Experiences Include:

Registered Professional Geologist specializing in groundwater and well drilling, holding license to consult and technical qualifications to render professional opinions on groundwater.

- Licensed well drilling contractor responsible for drilling shared wells.
- Licensed pump installing contractor who built many well systems sharing groundwater.
- Registered Geologist writing technical specifications for other well drillers/installers to construct shared water systems.
- Water well inspector for real estate sales who inspected many groundwater-sharing systems.
- Water well inspector for shared well buyers who explained agreement terms.

- Certified Real Estate instructor who taught real estate professionals and lenders essential aspects of Groundwater-Sharing Agreements.
- Expert Witness who testified several times in courts over disputes in well share agreements.
- Title examiner who authenticated and abstracted recorded documents and plotted/mapped legal descriptions of land to determine coverage of recorded agreements over parcels.

As far as known, authorship belongs solely to books on groundwater-sharing. If not an expert on groundwater-sharing, no one else qualifies.

Author Gary L. Hix

Resources and References

A Guide for Operating Shared Water Wells in Arizona, U of A Coop Ext. Bulletin 1810, Feb. 2020, G. Hix, et al.

A Primer on Groundwater Law, Joseph W. Dellapenna, 49 Idaho Law Review. 265 (2013).

Advocate Article: Drafting Key Provisions of a Shared Well Agreement, Arthur B. Macomber, Macomber Law PLLC.

An Arizona Well Owners Guide to Water Quality and Uses U of A Press, Jan. 2014, J. Artiola, G. Hix, et al.

Comparison of Groundwater Rights in the US a Lesson for Texas, Sanjaya Raj Joshi, Texas Tech Univ. MS Thesis. 2005.

Domestic Water Wells in Arizona, A Guide for Real Estate Professionals, E-Book, Amazon, 2016, G. Hix.

Existing Regulation of Exempt Wells in the United States, Jesse J. Richardson Jr. Univ. Council on Water Resources, Issue 148, 3-9, Aug. 2012.

Groundwater Well: Use and Shared Use Agreements, The Good, The Bad, and The Ugly, G. Hix, Lorman Education Services, Symposium, Tucson, AZ. Sept. 27, 2007.

HUD Handbook 4000.1, pages 186-191, 479, 573,602-604. Rev. Aug. 9, 2023.

National Groundwater Association (NGWA) Groundwater Facts. **www.ngwa.org**

Shared Water Wells in Arizona, A Guide for Well Managers, E-Book, Amazon 2019, G. Hix.

Two Tanks v. Rosas Water Co. Maricopa County Superior Court, 2016.

VA Pamphlet 26-7 Revised, Chapter 12 Minimum Property Requirements

Who Owns the Water? A publication of Water Systems Council, 2016.

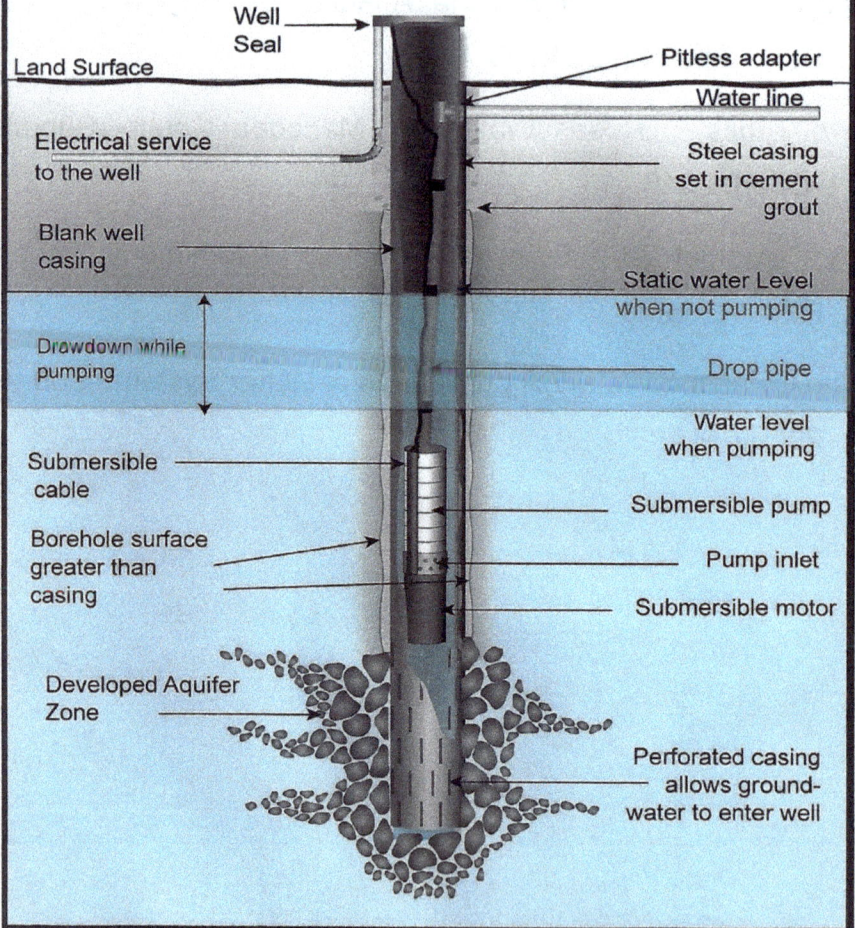

A Typical Modern Domestic Well a Pitless Adapter Completion.

Well Seal

Land Surface

Pitless adapter

Water line

Electrical service to the well

Steel casing set in cement grout

Blank well casing

Static water Level when not pumping

Drawdown while pumping

Drop pipe

Water level when pumping

Submersible cable

Submersible pump

Borehole surface greater than casing

Pump inlet

Submersible motor

Developed Aquifer Zone

Perforated casing allows groundwater to enter well

G.Hix 2026

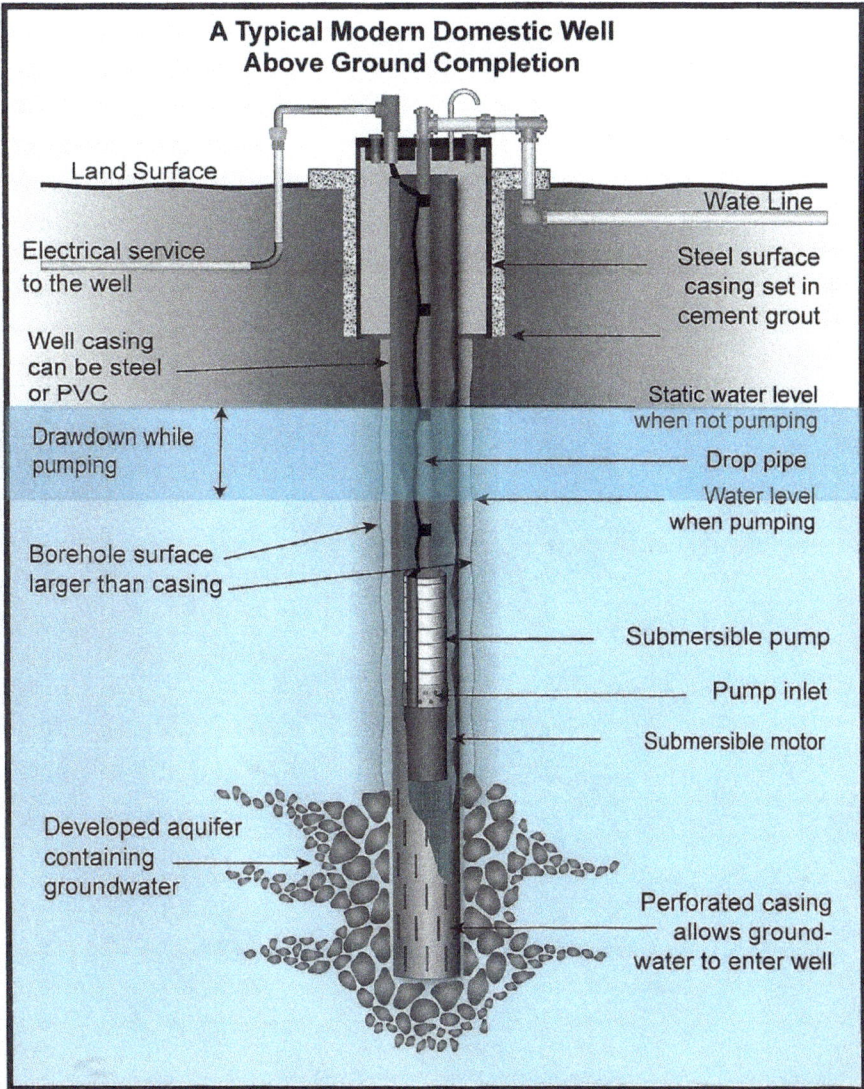

A Typical Modern Domestic Well
Above Ground Completion

Land Surface

Wate Line

Electrical service
to the well

Steel surface
casing set in
cement grout

Well casing
can be steel
or PVC

Static water level
when not pumping

Drawdown while
pumping

Drop pipe

Water level
when pumping

Borehole surface
larger than casing

Submersible pump

Pump inlet

Submersible motor

Developed aquifer
containing
groundwater

Perforated casing
allows ground-
water to enter well

G.Hix 2026

114